Woof!

Let's go
fly a CAT!

Are you in a "time-out"?

I thought you said these were Jimmy Chews.

Now you'll have to
take me with you ...
I ate the keys.

You want me to apologize
to the cat ... really?

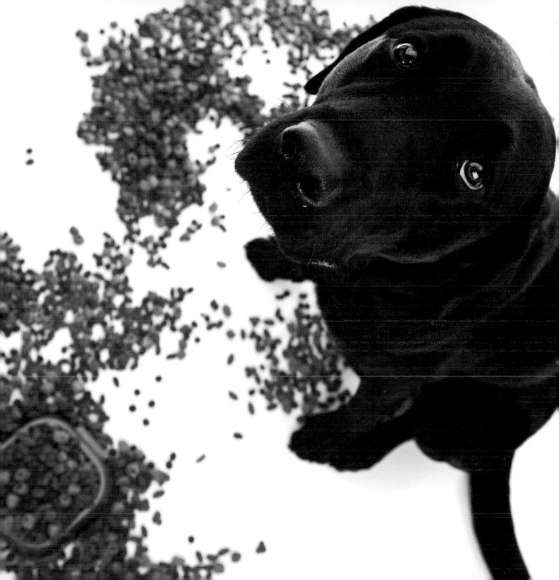

So many choices, so little time....

What cookie? I didn't hide a cookie. I don't know what you're talking about....

Sorry, I think I was sick the day they covered not doing this in obedience school.

Maybe this will make up
for what I did in the garden.

At least I didn't get my paw
caught in the cookie jar....

Nothing more embarrassing than getting your head caught in the cat door....

How many dogs does it take to
change a roll of toilet paper?
Yeah, I've heard that one before.

I'm not lying about that missing turkey leg.... What do you mean my nose is growing?

Hair on the couch? Not mine....

What does the fox say NOW?

Nobody knows the trouble I've been.

Would it help if I said I'm sorry?

Let's get outta here
before they realize we
raided their picnic basket!

I'm not pouting!

Delicious!

What smell?

I overheard you saying
your moisturizer helps with
age spots ... so I ate it.

I know. I have the
right to remain silent.

Everybody else is
sitting at the table....

Please don't hate me
because I'm beautiful!

I plead the Fifth.

Sister? I thought
she was a chew toy!

Do I look big enough to knock a trash can over and drag it through the house?

I swear I wore my
retainer every night!

Please don't send me
back to obedience school!

I'm meaner than a junkyard dog
before I have my first cup
of coffee in the morning.

I heard you the first time!
I won't do it again.

Can you really blame me
for biting the groomer?

Well, you put a slipcover on it,
so we thought it was ours now.

I just wanted to come with you.

What happens in Vegas...
stays in Vegas!

With special thanks to:
Jack Alexander, Jennifer Barney, Cary Cochrane, Kate Cochrane, Lisa Cochrane, Karen Hartman, Christopher Hiltz, Michael G. Ibrahim, Anne O'Connor, Maggie O'Connor, Frank Putrino, Anita Remijas, Barbara Rittenhouse, Mimi Roeder, Kathleen Rose, Ingrid Serio, Helene Shapiro, Patty Sprague, Linda Weber, Leslie Weyhrich

Additional photography: Shutterstock.com